meals in minutes

# easy vegetarian

**RECIPES**
Dana Jacobi

**PHOTOGRAPHS**
Bill Bettencourt

weldon**owen**

# contents

# about this book

Meals in Minutes *Easy Vegetarian* offers hearty, delicious recipes that anyone can enjoy. Making use of fresh, seasonal produce and bold spices from around the world, these innovative dishes present a healthy alternative for dinner. The majority of the recipes in this book can be prepared and on the table in under 30 minutes. Creamy Wild Mushroom Risotto with Peas is perfect for quick, hearty weeknight suppers. Recipes such as Roasted Root Vegetables with Sage Butter require only 15 minutes hands-on time, giving you more free time while dinner is in the oven.

Make a large batch of Spicy Tomato Sauce to serve over pasta tonight and have plenty of sauce for recipes such as Polenta Lasagna or Eggplant Parmesan later in the week. You will also find suggestions and tips on planning ahead, selecting and storing fresh vegetables, and preparing quick and easy side dishes to round out your meal—tools that will help you become a more organized, smarter cook.

# 30 minutes
## start to finish

# edamame, corn & tomato salad

**Fresh corn kernels,** 2 ears, or frozen corn kernels, ¾ cup (5 oz/155 g)

**Frozen shelled edamame,** 1½ cups (9 oz/280 g)

**Cherry tomatoes,** 12, halved

**Avocado,** 1 large, pitted, peeled, and cubed

**Fresh lime juice,** 2 tablespoons

**Salt and freshly ground pepper**

**Canola oil,** 1 tablespoon

**Romaine (cos) lettuce,** 8 dark outer leaves

**Fresh cilantro (fresh coriander),** 2 tablespoons chopped

SERVES 4

1 **Cook the corn and edamame**
Bring a saucepan of water to a boil and have ready a bowl of ice water. Add the corn and the edamame and cook for 3 minutes. Using a slotted spoon, transfer to the bowl of ice water. Drain the corn and edamame, place in a large bowl and add the tomatoes and avocado.

2 **Assemble the salad**
In a small bowl, whisk together the lime juice, 1 teaspoon salt, and ⅛ teaspoon pepper. Slowly whisk in the oil. Pour the dressing over the salad and gently toss to combine. Arrange the lettuce leaves on a serving platter and spoon the salad onto the leaves. Garnish with the cilantro and serve.

## cook's tip

Edamame is the Japanese word for soybean. Edamame makes a delicious and healthy snack, the pods are lightly boiled in water, salted, and the seeds are squeezed directly from the pods.

## cook's tip

Be sure to choose a good-quality
ricotta cheese. For the best results,
place a cheesecloth (muslin)
or paper towel-lined sieve over
a large measuring cup or bowl
and drain the ricotta of any
excess moisture.

# pappardelle with zucchini & lemon

## 1 Make the sauce

Bring a large pot of water to a boil. In a frying pan over medium-high heat, warm the oil. Add the shallot and sauté until translucent, about 2 minutes. Add the zucchini and ½ teaspoon salt and cook, stirring occasionally, until the zucchini is tender-crisp, 4–5 minutes. Remove from the heat and stir in the ricotta and lemon zest.

## 2 Cook the pasta

Meanwhile, add 2 tablespoons salt and the pasta to the boiling water. Cook, stirring occasionally to prevent sticking, until al dente, according to the package directions. Drain, reserving about ½ cup (4 fl oz/125 ml) of the cooking water. Add the pasta to the sauce and toss to combine. Add as much of the cooking water as needed to loosen the sauce. Divide the pasta among bowls and serve, passing the grated cheese at the table.

**Olive oil,** 1 tablespoon

**Shallot,** 1, minced

**Zucchini (courgettes),** 2, halved lengthwise and thinly sliced

**Salt and freshly ground pepper**

**Fresh ricotta cheese,** ¾ cup (6 oz/185 g)

**Zest from 1 lemon,** finely grated

**Pappardelle or wide egg noodles,** 1 lb (500 g)

**Pecorino or Parmesan cheese,** ½ cup (2 oz/60 g) freshly grated

SERVES 4

# red pepper & goat cheese frittata

**Olive oil,** 3 tablespoons

**Yellow onion,** 1, thinly sliced

**Roasted red pepper (capsicum),** ⅔ cup (4 oz/125 g) chopped

**Eggs,** 8

**Fresh oregano,** 2 tablespoons chopped

**Salt and freshly ground pepper**

**Fresh goat cheese,** 3 oz (90 g), crumbled

SERVES 4

1 Cook the vegetables
In a heavy 10-inch (25-cm) ovenproof frying pan over medium heat, warm the oil. Add the onion and sauté until golden, 5–6 minutes. Add the red pepper and cook, stirring, until warmed through, 1–2 minutes.

2 Prepare the frittata
While the vegetables are cooking, in a bowl, whisk together the eggs, oregano, ½ teaspoon salt, and ¼ teaspoon pepper. Spread the vegetables evenly in the pan, and then pour in the egg mixture. Reduce the heat to medium-low and cook, without stirring, until the edges begin to look set, about 3 minutes. Using a spatula, carefully lift up the edges of the frittata and let the uncooked egg run underneath. Continue to cook, without stirring, until the eggs are almost set on top, 5–8 minutes longer.

3 Finish the frittata
While the frittata is cooking, preheat the broiler (grill). Sprinkle the frittata with the goat cheese and place under the broiler. Broil (grill) until the top is set and the cheese is melted, about 2 minutes. Cut into large wedges and serve directly from the pan.

## cook's tip

Sautéing fresh mushrooms
in a dry frying pan over
medium-high heat helps
draw out their moisture and
concentrate the flavor. After
the mushrooms release their
juices, cook them further
to evaporate the liquid.

# linguine with creamy mushroom sauce

### 1 Make the sauce

Bring a large pot of water to a boil. In a frying pan, warm the oil over medium-high heat. Add the mushrooms and sauté until they have released most of their liquid, about 5 minutes. Stir in the garlic and thyme and cook, stirring, until the mushrooms are golden, 4–5 minutes more. Add the vermouth and cook, stirring until the alcohol has evaporated, about 2 minutes. Season to taste with salt and pepper and remove from the heat.

### 2 Cook the pasta

Meanwhile, add 2 tablespoons salt and the pasta to the boiling water. Cook, stirring occasionally to prevent sticking, until al dente, according to the package directions. Drain, reserving about ½ cup (4 fl oz/125 ml) of the cooking water. Add the pasta to the sauce along with the sour cream and cayenne. Stir to combine. Warm briefly over low heat to blend the flavors. Add as much of the cooking water as needed to loosen the sauce. Stir in the parsley, and serve.

**Olive oil,** 2 tablespoons

**Button mushrooms,** 6 oz (185 g), thinly sliced

**Cremini mushrooms,** 6 oz (185 g), thinly sliced

**Garlic,** 1–2 cloves, minced

**Dried thyme,** ½ teaspoon

**Dry vermouth,** or dry white wine, ¼ cup (2 fl oz/60 ml)

**Salt and freshly ground black pepper**

**Linguine,** 1 lb (500 g)

**Sour cream,** ½ cup (4 oz/ 125 g)

**Cayenne pepper,** pinch

**Fresh flat-leaf (Italian) parsley,** 2 tablespoons, chopped

SERVES 4

# creamy
# cauliflower gratin

**Cauliflower,** 1 large head, cut into 1-inch (2.5-cm) florets

**Salt and freshly ground pepper**

**Milk,** 2 cups (16 fl oz/ 500 ml)

**Unsalted butter,** 2 tablespoons

**Flour,** 2 tablespoons

**Dry mustard,** 1 teaspoon

**White cheddar cheese,** ½ cup (2 oz/60 g) shredded

**Gouda cheese,** ½ cup (2 oz/60 g) shredded

**Cayenne pepper,** pinch

**Dried bread crumbs,** 3 tablespoons

SERVES 4

## 1 Cook the cauliflower

Bring a large pot of water to a boil. Add the cauliflower and 1 tablespoon salt to the boiling water. Cook until the florets are tender, about 7 minutes. Drain well.

## 2 Make the sauce

In a small saucepan over medium heat, warm the milk until small bubbles begin to form around the edge of the pan. Remove from the heat. In a large saucepan over low heat, melt the butter. Add the flour and mustard a little at a time, whisking to incorporate. Raise the heat to medium-low and gradually whisk in the hot milk. Cook, stirring frequently, until the mixture is thick and creamy, about 5 minutes. Add the cheeses, salt and pepper to taste, and the cayenne. Cook, stirring frequently, until the cheeses are melted, about 2 minutes.

## 3 Finish the gratin

Preheat the broiler (grill) and butter a shallow 2-qt (2-l) gratin or baking dish. Arrange the cauliflower in the dish, pour the sauce over it and sprinkle with the bread crumbs. Broil (grill) until golden brown, about 2 minutes. Serve immediately.

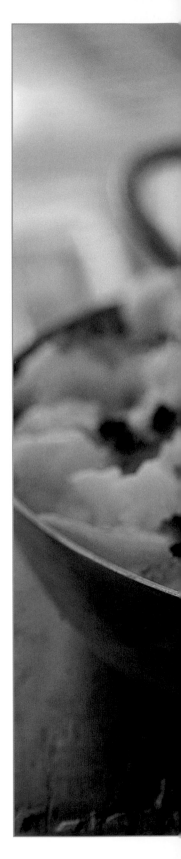

# penne with greens & pine nuts

## cook's tip

Toast pine nuts in a dry heavy-bottomed frying pan over medium-low heat, shaking the pan frequently, for about 5 minutes.

Or, spread them evenly on a baking sheet and place in a 350°F (180°C) oven for 10–12 minutes. The nuts are done when they are golden brown and fragrant.

### 1 Cook the greens

Bring a large pot of water to a boil. In a deep frying pan over medium-high heat, warm the oil. Add the onion and sauté until translucent, about 4 minutes. Add the garlic and cook, stirring often, until fragrant, about 2 minutes. Working in batches if necessary, add in the chard and kale and stir until wilted, about 4 minutes. Add ½ cup (4 fl oz/125 ml) water, cover, reduce the heat to medium, and cook, stirring occasionally, until the greens are tender-crisp, 10–15 minutes. Stir in the raisins and nuts and remove from the heat.

### 2 Cook the pasta

Meanwhile, add 2 tablespoons salt and the pasta to the boiling water. Cook, stirring occasionally to prevent sticking, until al dente, according to the package directions. Drain, reserving about ½ cup (4 fl oz/125 ml) of the cooking water. Add as much of the cooking water as needed to the sauce and toss to combine. Divide among shallow bowls, and serve.

**Olive oil,** 2 tablespoons

**Red onion,** 1 large, chopped

**Garlic,** 2 cloves, minced

**Swiss chard,** 1 lb (500 g), ribs removed and leaves chopped

**Kale,** ½ bunch, stems removed and leaves chopped

**Golden raisins (sultanas),** ¼ cup (1½ oz/45 oz)

**Pine nuts,** ¼ cup (1½ oz/45 g), toasted

**Salt and freshly ground pepper**

**Penne,** 1 lb (500 g)

SERVES 4

21

# asparagus milanese

**Asparagus,** 1 lb (500 g), ends trimmed

**Unsalted butter,** 2 tablespoons

**Eggs,** 4

**Salt and freshly ground pepper**

**Shallot,** 1 tablespoon minced

**Panko or fresh bread crumbs,** 2 tablespoons

SERVES 4

1 Steam the asparagus
Fill a frying pan with 1 inch (2.5 cm) of water and bring to a boil. Add the asparagus, cover, and cook until bright green and tender-crisp, 3–4 minutes. Drain and divide the asparagus among 4 plates. Wipe out the pan.

2 Cook the eggs
In the same pan over medium heat, melt the butter. Carefully break each egg into the pan. Season to taste with salt and pepper. Cook until the whites and yolks are set, about 4 minutes. Using a wide spatula, place one egg on each serving of asparagus. Add the shallot and panko to the pan and sauté until the crumbs are golden, about 2 minutes. Sprinkle over the eggs and serve immediately.

## cook's tip

Whenever you have leftover
day-old bread, preferably
a baguette or rustic white loaf,
cut it into slices, place on a baking
sheet, and dry out the slices
in the oven at 300°F (150°C) for
about 10 minutes. Process the
toasted bread in a food processor
to make crumbs. Store the crumbs
in an airtight container in the
freezer for up to 4 months.

## cook's tip

Also called bean curd, tofu
is sold in blocks with textures
ranging from silken to extra-firm.
Firm tofu holds its shape when
stir-fried. Soft, silken tofu is best
gently cooked in recipes such
as soups. Before using tofu, drain
it, rinse briefly, and drain again.

# tofu stir-fry with black bean sauce

## 1 Prepare the tofu and sauce

Line a baking sheet with a double thickness of paper towels. Arrange the tofu in a single layer on the towels. Top with another layer of towels and pat the tofu dry. In a small bowl, stir together the cornstarch and broth until the cornstarch dissolves. Stir in the bean sauce and sugar and set aside.

## 2 Stir-fry the vegetables

Heat a wok or large frying pan over high heat and add the oil. Carefully add the tofu and cook for 3 minutes. Turn and continue to cook until golden, 3–4 minutes. Using a slotted spoon, transfer to paper towels to drain. Pour off all but 1 tablespoon oil and place the wok over high heat. Add the pepper flakes, bok choy, zucchini, bell pepper, and snap peas and stir-fry until the vegetables are tender-crisp, about 3 minutes. Return the tofu to the wok. Stir in the sauce and cook, stirring, until the sauce thickens, about 1 minute. Serve in shallow bowls.

**Firm tofu,** 1 lb (500 g), cut into ¾-inch (2-cm) cubes

**Cornstarch (cornflour),** 1 tablespoon

**Vegetable broth,** ¼ cup (2 fl oz/60 ml)

**Black bean sauce,** 1 tablespoon

**Sugar,** 1 teaspoon

**Peanut oil,** ⅓ cup (3 fl oz/80 ml)

**Red pepper flakes,** ⅛ teaspoon

**Bok choy,** 1 small head, trimmed and cut into 1-inch (2.5-cm) pieces

**Green or yellow zucchini (courgette),** 1 small, cut into slices ¾ inch (2 cm) thick

**Red bell pepper (capsicum),** 1, seeded and chopped

**Sugar snap peas,** ¼ lb (125 g), trimmed

SERVES 4

# miso soup
# with udon noodles

**Udon noodles,** 1 lb (500 g)

**Vegetable broth,** 4 cups
(32 fl oz/1 l)

**Fresh ginger,** 3 thin slices

**Sake,** 2 tablespoons

**Red miso,** 2 tablespoons

**Silken tofu,** ¼ lb (125 g),
cut into ½-inch (12-mm)
cubes

**Button mushrooms,** 2 large,
thinly sliced

**Carrot,** 1 small, thinly sliced

**Green (spring) onion,**
1 large, dark green part only,
thinly sliced lengthwise

SERVES 4

## 1 Cook the noodles

Fill a large pot half-full with water and bring to a boil.
Add the noodles and return the water to a boil. Cook until the
noodles are al dente, 2–3 minutes. Drain the noodles, rinse
well under cold running water, and drain again. Divide among
4 soup bowls.

## 2 Make the soup

In a medium saucepan over medium-high heat, warm
the broth with the ginger and sake until bubbles begin to form
around the edge of the pan. Reduce heat to medium-low and
simmer 5 minutes to infuse the flavors. Remove the ginger.
Place the miso in a small bowl and add ¼ cup (2 fl oz/60 ml)
of the hot broth. Stir until the miso is dissolved and creamy,
and pour the mixture back into the pot. Place the tofu in a sieve
and warm it under a slow stream of hot running water. Divide
the tofu among the soup bowls. Ladle in the hot broth, dividing
it among the bowls. Garnish with the sliced mushrooms,
carrot, and green onion, and serve.

## cook's tip

Miso, a savory, highly
nutritional fermented paste
made from soybeans, comes
in many colors, thicknesses,
and varieties. If you cannot

find red miso, you may
substitute white miso, also
known as *shiromiso*, and
is available in Japanese
groceries, and well-stocked
supermarkets.

## cook's tip

When refrigerated, leftovers
of this curry will thicken
considerably. To reheat, you
may need to add a little
water or vegetable broth and
warm it, covered, over
medium heat just until hot.

# chickpea & sweet potato curry

1 **Make the curry base**
In a heavy-bottomed saucepan over medium-low heat, warm the oil. Add the onion, garlic, ginger, and chile and cook, stirring occasionally, until the onion is translucent, about 4 minutes. Stir in the curry powder and cook, stirring constantly, until fragrant, about 30 seconds. Season to taste with salt and pepper.

2 **Cook the vegetables**
Add the sweet potato, chickpeas, the coconut milk, and 1 cup (8 fl oz/250 ml) water to the pan. Raise the heat to medium-high, bring just to a boil, reduce the heat, and simmer, uncovered, until the sweet potato is tender, about 10 minutes. Add the peas and tomatoes and cook until heated through. Serve in bowls over steamed rice, if desired.

**Canola oil,** 2 tablespoons

**Yellow onion,** 1 small, chopped

**Garlic,** 2 cloves, finely chopped

**Fresh ginger,** 1 tablespoon chopped

**Thai or jalapeño chile,** 1, seeded and finely chopped

**Curry powder,** 1 tablespoon

**Salt and freshly ground pepper**

**Sweet potato,** 1 large, peeled and cut into ½-inch (12-mm) cubes

**Chickpeas (garbanzo beans),** 1 can (15 oz/470 g), drained and rinsed

**Coconut milk,** 1 can (about 14 fl oz/400 ml), well shaken

**Frozen peas,** ½ cup (2½ oz/ 75 g)

**Canned diced tomatoes,** ½ cup (3 fl oz/80 ml) drained

**Steamed basmati rice,** for serving (optional)

SERVES 4

# polenta with vegetable ragout

**Olive oil,** 4 tablespoons
(2 fl oz/60 ml)

**Garlic,** 2 cloves, chopped

**Asian (slender) eggplant
(aubergine),** 1 small, halved
lengthwise and sliced

**Red bell pepper
(capsicum),** 1, seeded and
sliced crosswise into strips

**Zucchini (courgette),**
1 small, halved lengthwise and
thinly sliced

**Fresh thyme,** 1 tablespoon
chopped

**Canned whole plum
(Roma) tomatoes,** 2½ cups
(20 fl oz/625 ml), with juice

**Vegetable broth,** 4 cups
(32 fl oz/1 l)

**Salt and freshly ground
pepper**

**Quick-cooking polenta,**
1 cup (7 oz/220 g)

SERVES 4

1 Make the ragout
In a large frying pan over medium heat, warm
3 tablespoons of the oil. Add the garlic, eggplant, bell pepper,
zucchini, and thyme and cook, stirring occasionally, until the
vegetables begin to soften, about 5 minutes. Add the tomatoes
and ¼ cup (2 fl oz/60 ml) water and cook until the vegetables
are soft but still hold their shape, 8–10 minutes, stirring
occasionally to break up the tomatoes.

2 Cook the polenta
In a deep saucepan, bring the broth to a boil. Add
1 tablespoon salt. Gradually whisk in the polenta. Reduce the
heat to medium-low and cook, stirring frequently, until the
polenta is thick and soft, 5–8 minutes. Remove the pan from
the heat and season to taste with salt and pepper. Divide
the polenta among bowls, top with the ragout, and serve.

## cook's tip

It's best to avoid using
purchased vegetable broth
that lists carrots as the first
ingredient. This gives finished
dishes an orange cast. If you
do not have vegetable broth,
substitute water and add
⅓ cup (1½ oz/45 g) freshly
grated Parmesan cheese.

## cook's tip

For a heartier salad mix 1 cup
(5 oz/125 g) crumbled feta
cheese into the bulgur and serve
with warm toasted pita bread.

# greek bulgur salad

## 1 Prepare the bulgur

Bring 3 cups (24 fl oz/750 ml) water to a boil. Place the bulgur in a bowl, pour in the boiling water, and set aside until the bulgur is soft, about 20 minutes. Drain the bulgur in a fine-mesh sieve and return to the bowl. Add the lemon juice, oil, garlic, 1/2 teaspoon salt, and 1/8 teaspoon pepper, and stir well. Stir in the mint, tomatoes, and cucumber.

## 2 Assemble the salad

Line a serving platter with the lettuce leaves or divide among 4 salad plates. Mound the bulgur salad on top of the lettuce and serve.

**Bulgur,** 1 cup (6 oz/185 g)

**Fresh lemon juice,** 2 tablespoons

**Olive oil,** 1 tablespoon

**Garlic,** 1 small clove, minced

**Salt and freshly ground pepper**

**Fresh mint,** 3/4 cup (1 oz/ 30 g) chopped

**Cherry tomatoes,** 2 cups (12 oz/375 g) halved

**Cucumber,** 1 small, peeled, seeded, and cut into 1/2-inch (12-mm) cubes

**Romaine (cos) lettuce,** 4 large leaves

SERVES 4

# wild mushroom risotto with peas

**Dried porcini mushrooms,** ¼ oz (7 g), about 2 tablespoons, rinsed

**Vegetable broth,** 5½ cups (44 fl oz/1.35 l)

**Dry white wine,** 1 cup (8 fl oz/250 ml)

**Unsalted butter,** 1 tablespoon

**Olive oil,** 1 tablespoon

**Yellow onion,** 1 small, finely chopped

**Arborio rice,** 2 cups (14 oz/440 g)

**Frozen peas,** 1 cup (5 oz/155 g)

**Parmesan cheese,** ½ cup (2 oz/60 g) freshly grated, plus shards for garnish

**Salt and freshly ground pepper**

SERVES 4

### 1 Prepare the mushrooms

Place the mushrooms in a small bowl. Add ⅓ cup (3 fl oz/80 ml) hot water and let stand until the mushrooms are soft, about 20 minutes. Drain and finely chop the mushrooms.

### 2 Cook the rice

Meanwhile, in a saucepan over medium heat, bring the broth and wine to a gentle simmer, then maintain the simmer over low heat. Meanwhile, in a heavy-bottomed saucepan or Dutch oven over medium heat, melt the butter with the oil. Add the onion and sauté until softened, about 4 minutes. Add the rice and cook, stirring constantly, until the grains are opaque and well coated, about 1 minute. Add 2 cups (16 fl oz/500 ml) of the simmering broth mixture and cook, stirring frequently, until the liquid is absorbed, 3–4 minutes. Reduce the heat to medium-low and continue to add the broth 1 cup (8 fl oz/250 ml) at a time, stirring occasionally, and adding more only after the previous addition has been absorbed.

### 3 Finish the risotto

When the rice is tender and creamy, but still al dente, after about 20 minutes, stir in the mushrooms and peas and cook for 2 minutes. Stir in the ½ cup Parmesan cheese. Season to taste with salt and pepper, and serve in shallow bowls garnished with the shards of cheese.

## cook's tip

Adjust the heat in this dish
to your taste by reducing
or increasing the amount of chili
paste or even by eliminating
it. If you do not have chili paste
such as Sriracha, red pepper
flakes or cayenne pepper may
be substituted.

# peanut-braised
# tofu with noodles

### 1 Prepare the tofu

Line a baking sheet with a double thickness of paper towels. Arrange the tofu in a single layer on the towels. Top with another layer of towels and pat the tofu dry.

### 2 Cook the vegetables and noodles

Bring a large pot of water to a boil. Add the snow peas, cook for 30 seconds, remove with a slotted spoon and set aside. Add the noodles to the boiling water and cook according to the package directions. Drain the noodles, rinse well under cold running water, and drain again. Set aside.

### 3 Braise the tofu

In a saucepan over medium heat, stir together the coconut milk and peanut butter until well combined. Stir in the chili paste, sugar, broth, soy sauce, and lime juice. Add the tofu. Cook, stirring occasionally, until the sauce is hot and the tofu is heated through, about 2 minutes. Stir in the peas and the noodles. Divide among bowls, and serve.

**Firm tofu,** 1 lb (500 g), cut into ¾-inch (2-cm) cubes

**Snow peas (mangetouts),** 1 cup, trimmed and cut in half

**Thin fresh Chinese noodles,** ½ lb (250 g)

**Coconut milk,** ½ cup (4 fl oz/125 ml)

**Creamy peanut butter,** ½ cup (5 oz/155 g)

**Chili paste,** 1 tablespoon

**Sugar,** 1 teaspoon

**Vegetable broth,** ¼ cup (2 fl oz/60 ml)

**Soy sauce,** 2 tablespoons

**Fresh lime juice,** 2 tablespoons

SERVES 4

# spicy corn cakes with black beans

**Black beans,** 1 can (15 oz/ 470 g), drained

**Fresh oregano**, 1 teaspoon chopped

**Chili powder,** 2 teaspoons

**Stone ground yellow cornmeal,** ²⁄₃ cup (3 oz/ 90 g)

**Flour,** 2 tablespoons

**Baking soda (bicarbonate of soda),** ¼ teaspoon

**Salt and freshly ground pepper**

**Unsalted butter,** 3 tablespoons, melted

**Buttermilk,** 1 cup (8 fl oz/250 ml)

**Egg,** 1

**Frozen corn kernels,** ½ cup (3 oz/90 g), thawed

**Canola oil,** 2 teaspoons

SERVES 4

1 **Prepare the beans**
In a saucepan over medium heat, stir together the beans, oregano, and 1 teaspoon of the chili powder. Cook, stirring occasionally, until the beans are heated through. Remove from the heat, cover, and set aside.

2 **Make the batter**
In a bowl, whisk together the cornmeal, flour, baking soda, the remaining 1 teaspoon chili powder, ½ teaspoon salt, and ⅛ teaspoon pepper. In another bowl, whisk together the butter, buttermilk, and egg until well combined. Mix the liquid ingredients quickly into the dry ingredients until just blended, leaving small lumps. Fold in the corn.

3 **Make the pancakes**
Heat a large cast-iron frying pan over medium-high heat. Brush it with 1 teaspoon of the oil. Working in batches, add the batter, ¼ cup (2 fl oz/60 ml) at a time. Cook the pancakes until they are browned and puffy, about 4 minutes, turning once. Transfer to a plate and cover loosely with aluminum foil. Stir the batter and wipe the pan with oil between batches. Divide the pancakes among plates. Spoon the beans over the cakes and serve.

## cook's tip

For even more flavor, top corn cakes with sour cream, purchased or homemade salsa, and chopped cilantro (fresh coriander). To make a quick homemade salsa combine 1 tomato, seeded and chopped; ½ onion, chopped; 2 tablespoons chopped cilantro (fresh coriander); and fresh lime juice to taste.

## cook's tip

For heartier fare, serve with hard-cooked eggs. Bring eggs to a boil in a small saucepan, cover and cook for 10 minutes. Remove

from the heat, run under cold water and set aside to cool. Eggs can be cooked up to 2 days in advance and kept in the refrigerator for later use.

# mediterranean potato salad

## 1 Cook the beans and potatoes

Bring a large pot of water to a boil. Add 1 tablespoon salt and the green beans and cook until bright green and tender-crisp, about 3 minutes. Using a slotted spoon, transfer to a bowl of ice water. Drain the beans and place in a large bowl. Add the potatoes to the boiling water and cook until almost tender, about 10 minutes, and drain. Add the potatoes to the beans.

## 2 Assemble the salad

Add the chickpeas, onion, parsley, mint, olives, and capers to the green beans and potatoes. In a small bowl, whisk together the mustard, vinegar, 1 teaspoon salt, and ⅛ teaspoon pepper. Whisk in the oil. Pour the dressing over the salad and toss until well coated, then serve.

**Salt and freshly ground pepper**

**Thin green beans,** ¼ lb (125 g), trimmed

**Red-skinned potatoes,** 1 ¼ lb (625 g), quartered

**Canned chickpeas (garbanzo beans) or kidney beans,** 1 cup (7 oz/220 g) drained and rinsed

**Red onion,** 1 small, finely chopped

**Fresh flat-leaf (Italian) parsley,** ½ cup (¾ oz/20 g) roughly chopped

**Fresh mint,** ½ cup (¾ oz/ 20 g) roughly chopped

**Sicilian or other green olives,** 4, pitted and coarsely chopped

**Capers,** 1 tablespoon, rinsed and chopped

**Whole-grain mustard,** 1 tablespoon

**Red wine vinegar,** 1 tablespoon

**Olive oil,** 1 tablespoon

SERVES 4

# sweet potato hash with poached eggs

**Red-skinned potato,**
1 large (½ lb/250 g), peeled and cut into ¾-inch (2-cm) cubes

**Sweet potato,** 1 (½ lb/ 250 g), peeled and cut into ¾-inch (2-cm) cubes

**Canola oil,** 2 tablespoons

**Red bell pepper (capsicum),** 1 small, seeded and chopped

**Red onion,** 1 small, finely chopped

**Green (spring) onion,** 1, white and dark green parts, chopped

**Salt and freshly ground pepper**

**White distilled vinegar,** 1 tablespoon

**Eggs,** 4

SERVES 4

1 **Cook the potatoes**
Place the potatoes in a medium saucepan and cover with cold water. Bring the water to a boil, reduce the heat to medium-high and cook until the potatoes are almost tender, about 10 minutes. Drain well and set aside.

2 **Assemble the hash**
Meanwhile, warm the oil in a large frying pan over medium-high heat. Add the pepper and red onion and sauté until the red onion is translucent, about 2 minutes. Add the potatoes, spreading them in one layer. Reduce the heat to medium and cook, stirring occasionally, until the potatoes start to brown and the peppers are soft, about 6 minutes. Stir in the green onion. Season to taste with salt and pepper and cook, stirring until the potatoes start to break down and the green onion is softened, about 1 minute. Divide the hash among serving plates.

3 **Poach the eggs**
Meanwhile, in a deep sauté pan, bring 8 cups (64 fl oz/2 l) water to a gentle simmer over medium heat. Mix in the vinegar and 1 teaspoon salt. One at a time, crack the eggs into a small bowl then slide them into the water. After 1 minute, slip a spatula under the eggs to prevent them from sticking to the bottom. Cook the eggs 3–4 minutes. Using a slotted spoon, carefully remove the eggs from the water and place on top of each serving of hash, and serve.

## cook's tip

For the best results, use cold eggs taken directly from the refrigerator, as their whites are thicker than those of room-temperature eggs. Using a spoon, gently swirl the water around each egg as the whites set in the water.

## cook's tip

Portobello burgers can be made with a variety of toppings. In place of the Monterey Jack cheese and tomatoes, use roasted red peppers (capsicums) and fresh goat cheese. Simply spread the goat cheese on one side of each toasted bun.

# grilled portobello burgers

## 1 Cook the mushrooms

Prepare a gas or charcoal grill for direct grilling over medium-high heat, or preheat a stovetop grill pan. In a small bowl, stir together the oil, vinegar, garlic, ½ teaspoon salt, and ⅛ teaspoon pepper. Using a small spoon, remove the gills from the underside of the mushrooms. Brush both sides of the mushrooms with the oil mixture. Place the mushrooms on the grill stem side up and cook until well marked, about 4 minutes. Turn and cook until tender, about 4 minutes longer. Place one slice of cheese on top of each mushroom 2 minutes before you remove them from the grill and cook until melted.

## 2 Toast the rolls

Meanwhile, cut the rolls in half horizontally. Place each half, cut side down, on the cooler part of the grill until lightly toasted, 2–3 minutes. Alternatively, use a toaster oven.

## 3 Assemble the burgers

In a small bowl, mix together the pesto and mayonnaise and season to taste with salt and pepper. Spread the pesto-mayonnaise on the toasted rolls. Place a grilled mushroom on the bottom of each roll and top with the tomato slices. Top with the top half of the roll, and serve.

**Olive oil,** 2 tablespoons

**Balsamic vinegar,** 1 tablespoon

**Garlic,** 1 clove, minced

**Salt and freshly ground pepper**

**Portobello mushrooms,** 4 large, stems removed

**Monterey Jack cheese or smoked mozzarella,** cut into 4 slices

**Round Italian rolls,** 4

**Pesto,** 2 tablespoons (1 fl oz/30 ml), purchased

**Mayonnaise,** ½ cup, (4 fl oz/125 ml)

**Tomato,** 1–2 sliced

SERVES 4

# spanish bean stew

**Olive oil,** 3 tablespoons

**Yellow onion,** 1 large, chopped

**Vegetable broth,** 2 cups (16 fl oz/500 ml)

**Carrot,** 1 small, chopped

**Leek,** 1, white part only, halved, rinsed, and coarsely chopped

**Spanish or Hungarian paprika,** 2 teaspoons

**Garlic,** 2 large cloves, chopped

**Green beans,** ½ lb (300 g), trimmed and cut into 1-inch (2.5-cm) pieces

**Kidney or pinto beans,** 2 cans (15 oz/470 g), rinsed and drained

**Salt and freshly ground pepper**

SERVES 4

## 1 Prepare the onions

In a heavy-bottomed saucepan or Dutch oven over medium-high heat, warm 2 tablespoons of the oil. Add the onion and sauté until soft and translucent, about 8 minutes. Remove from the heat and transfer half of the onion to a blender. Add the broth, process until smooth, and set aside.

## 2 Finish the stew

Return the pan to medium-high heat and heat the remaining 1 tablespoon oil. Add the carrot and leek to the remaining onion and sauté until the leek is tender, about 5 minutes. Reduce the heat to medium, stir in the paprika and garlic, and cook, stirring, for 1 minute. Add the green beans, kidney beans, and puréed onion, and cook, stirring occasionally, until the beans are tender-crisp, 8–10 minutes. Season to taste with salt and pepper, divide among soup bowls, and serve.

## cook's tip

Crostini are a great addition
to this stew and take only
minutes to prepare. To make
them, preheat the oven to 400°F
(200°C). Cut a baguette into
½-inch (12-mm) slices, brush
with olive oil, and place on
a baking sheet. Bake until golden,
about 5 minutes. Peel a clove
of garlic and rub it onto each
warm slice of bread. Serve
alongside or on top of the stew.

# 15 minutes
# hands-on time

# winter squash with spiced couscous

**Acorn squash,** 2, each
1 ¼ lb (750 g), halved, seeds
removed

**Olive oil,** 2 teaspoons

**Salt and freshly ground
pepper**

**Vegetable broth,** 1 cup
(8 fl oz/250 ml)

**Instant couscous,** ¾ cup
(4½ oz/140 g)

**Ground cinnamon,**
½ teaspoon

**Ground ginger,** ¼ teaspoon

**Sliced almonds,**
3 tablespoons, toasted

**Dried currants,**
2 tablespoons

**Green (spring) onions,**
2, white and green parts, finely
chopped

**Golden Delicious apple,**
½, cored and chopped

SERVES 4

1 Roast the squash
Preheat the oven to 400°F (200°C). Brush the squash halves with the oil and season to taste with salt and pepper. Place the halves, cut side down, on a baking sheet. Roast until a thin knife easily pierces the squash, about 20 minutes.

2 Make the spiced couscous
Meanwhile, in a saucepan, bring the broth to a boil. Stir in the couscous, cinnamon, ginger, ½ teaspoon salt, and pepper to taste. Cover and set aside, according to the package directions. Stir in the almonds, currants, onions, and apple into the couscous. Spoon the filling into the roasted squash, mounding it generously, and serve.

## cook's tip

Other small winter squash, such as butternut squash, will work well in this dish as the orange flesh is sweet and will be complemented by the spiced couscous. Simply cube the squash, roast in chunks, and stir into the cooked couscous. The roasting time will decrease by about 10 minutes.

# spring vegetable tart

### 1 Prepare the pastry

Preheat the oven to 400°F (200°C). Line a rimmed baking sheet with parchment (baking) paper. Lay the puff pastry on the baking sheet. Fold over the sides to make a 1-inch (2.5-cm) rim, overlapping the pastry at the corners and pressing it lightly. Inside the rim, prick the pastry all over with a fork.

### 2 Fill and bake the tart

Sprinkle half of the cheese over the bottom of the pastry inside the rim. Top with the asparagus, laying the spears vertically in a row from one side of the pastry to the other. Sprinkle the leeks over the asparagus. Bake for 15 minutes. Meanwhile, in a bowl, beat the eggs, milk, ½ teaspoon salt, and pepper to taste until well combined. Pour the egg mixture over the asparagus and leeks and sprinkle on the remaining cheese. Bake until the pastry is puffed and golden brown, about 10 minutes longer. Let the tart stand for 10 minutes. Cut into pieces and serve.

**Frozen puff pastry,** 1 sheet, thawed

**Fontina cheese,** 1 cup (4 oz/125 g) shredded

**Asparagus,** 15–20 thin spears, trimmed

**Leek,** 1 small, white part only, halved, rinsed, and thinly sliced

**Eggs,** 2

**Milk,** ¼ cup (2 fl oz/60 ml)

**Salt and freshly ground pepper**

SERVES 4

# potato & gruyère
## tartlets

Olive oil, 2 tablespoons

Fresh rosemary,
1 tablespoon finely chopped

Salt and freshly ground
pepper

Russet or baking potato,
1, peeled, halved lengthwise
and thinly sliced

Yellow onion, 1 small,
halved and thinly sliced

Frozen puff pastry,
1 sheet, thawed and cut into
four 5-inch (13-cm) squares

Gruyère cheese,
1 cup (4 oz/125 g) shredded

SERVES 4

1 Make the filling
Preheat the oven to 400°F (200°C). In a bowl, stir together the oil, rosemary, ½ teaspoon salt, and ⅛ teaspoon pepper. Add the potato and onion and toss to coat.

2 Prepare the pastry
Lay the pastry squares on a baking sheet. With a sharp paring knife cut a ½-inch (12-mm) border along the edge of the pastry, being careful not to cut more than halfway through. Inside the rim, prick the pastry all over with a fork.

3 Fill and bake the tartlets
Sprinkle 2 tablespoons of the cheese inside the rim of each tartlet. Divide the filling among the tartlet. Sprinkle the remaining cheese over the filling, dividing evenly. Bake until the rims are puffed and brown and the cheese is golden, about 20 minutes. Let the tartlets stand for 10 minutes. Serve warm or at room temperature.

## cook's tip

As a quick side dish, accompany the tartlets with steamed thin green beans. Bring a saucepan of lightly salted water to a boil, add the green beans and cook until tender-crisp, about 4 minutes. Run under cold water to cool.

# wild rice salad

## cook's tip

To peel and section an orange, cut a thin slice off the top and bottom. Set the orange on one end on a cutting board. Slice off

the peel in vertical strips, also cutting away the white pith. Holding the orange over a bowl to collect its juices, slide the knife down the membrane on either side of each section, and drop it into the bowl.

**1 Cook the rice**
In a large saucepan, place the rice, 3 cups (24 fl oz/750 ml) water and ½ teaspoon salt. Bring to a boil over medium-high heat. Reduce the heat to medium-low, cover, and simmer until the rice is just tender, about 40 minutes. Drain and place in a bowl.

**2 Assemble the salad**
Add the celery, cranberries, walnuts, oranges, and juice to the rice. Add the oil and stir with a fork to combine. Season to taste with salt and pepper. Spoon the salad into a serving bowl. Sprinkle with the pomegranate seeds, if using, and serve.

**Wild rice,** ¾ cup (4½ oz/140 g)

**Salt and freshly ground pepper**

**Celery,** 1 large stalk, chopped

**Dried cranberries,** ⅓ cup (2 oz/60 g)

**Walnuts,** ⅓ cup (2½ oz/75 g) chopped

**Orange,** 1–2, preferably Navel, peeled, sectioned, and chopped

**Fresh orange juice,** ¼ cup (2 fl oz/60 ml)

**Walnut or canola oil,** 1 tablespoon

**Pomegranate seeds,** ¼ cup (1 oz/30 g) (optional)

SERVES 4

# miso-glazed eggplant

**Peanut oil,** 2 tablespoons

**Asian (slender) eggplants (aubergines),** 4, halved lengthwise and crosswise

**White miso,** 3 tablespoons

**Mirin or sake,** 2 tablespoons

**Sugar,** 1 teaspoon

**Vegetable broth,** 2 tablespoons

**Asian sesame oil,** 1 teaspoon

**Sesame seeds,** 2 tablespoons

**Steamed rice,** for serving

SERVES 4

## 1 Prepare the eggplant

Preheat the oven to 375°F (190°C). Oil a baking dish just large enough to hold the eggplant in a single layer. In a large frying pan over medium-high heat, warm the peanut oil. Add the eggplant halves, cut side down, and cook until brown, about 5 minutes. Arrange the eggplants, with the cut side up, in the prepared dish.

## 2 Glaze and bake the eggplant

In a small bowl, mix the miso and mirin until creamy. Stir in the sugar, broth, and sesame oil. Spoon the glaze over the eggplants. Bake until the eggplants are soft yet still hold their shape and the glaze is bubbly and browned, about 25–30 minutes.

## 3 Toast the sesame seeds

Meanwhile, in a small, dry frying pan over medium-high heat, toast the sesame seeds, shaking the pan frequently, until they start to pop, about 5 minutes. Sprinkle on the glazed eggplants and serve with the rice.

## cook's tip

To spice up your steamed rice, stir in ¼ cup thinly sliced green (spring) onions and 1 tablespoon toasted sesame seeds.

## cook's tip

To protect your cutting board
from the red juice of the beets,
cover it with waxed paper
or plastic wrap. To avoid staining
your skin when peeling beets,
wear plastic sandwich bags over
your hands for protection.

# beet, fennel & arugula salad

**1 Roast the beets**
Preheat the oven to 400°F (200°C) and rub the beets with the 2 teaspoons oil. Wrap the beets individually in aluminum foil and bake until they are easily pierced with a knife, about 1 hour. Let cool to the touch in the foil. Peel and slice the beets.

**2 Make the dressing**
Meanwhile, in a large bowl, whisk together the vinegar, ½ teaspoon salt, and pepper to taste. Whisk in the 2 tablespoons oil.

**3 Assemble the salad**
Toss the arugula in the dressing until lightly coated. Divide among salad plates, shaking off any excess dressing. Using a vegetable peeler, shave the cheese generously over the greens. Toss the fennel in the dressing and then arrange on the greens. Toss the beets and the shallots in the dressing and then mound in the center of each serving.

**Beets,** 4, with 1 inch (2.5 cm) of stem intact

**Olive oil,** 2 teaspoons plus 2 tablespoons

**Sherry vinegar,** 2 tablespoons

**Salt and freshly ground pepper**

**Baby arugula (rocket),** 4 cups (4 oz/125 g)

**Manchego cheese,** 2 oz (60 g)

**Fennel bulb,** 1, cored, trimmed and cut into 8 wedges

**Shallot,** 1, thinly sliced

SERVES 4

61

# roasted vegetables with sage butter

**Golden or red beets,**
2, peeled and each cut into wedges

**Turnip,** 1, peeled, if desired, and cut into wedges

**Delicata or butternut squash,** 1, about 6 oz (185 g) peeled, seeded and cut into 1 inch (2.5 cm) chunks

**Fennel,** 1 small bulb, trimmed and cut into slices

**Parsnip,** 1, peeled and cut into chunks

**Baby carrots,** 8

**Garlic,** 4 cloves, halved lengthwise

**Unsalted butter,**
4 tablespoons (2 oz/60 g), melted

**Fresh sage,** 3 tablespoons chopped

**Salt and freshly ground pepper**

**White balsamic vinegar,**
1 tablespoon

SERVES 4

1 Roast the vegetables
Preheat the oven to 400°F (200°C). Place the beets, turnip, squash, fennel, parsnip, carrots, and garlic on a baking sheet. Pour the butter over the vegetables. Sprinkle with the sage, 1 teaspoon salt, and ¼ teaspoon pepper. Toss until the vegetables are coated, then spread in an even layer. Roast, stirring occasionally, about 30 minutes. Continue to roast, without stirring, until the vegetables are tender, 20–30 minutes longer. Using a large spatula, transfer the vegetables to a serving bowl. Reserve the pan juices.

2 Finish the vegetables
Pour any remaining pan juices into a small bowl and whisk in the vinegar. Drizzle over the vegetables, toss, and serve.

## cook's tip

Farro is an Italian variety of the grain also known as spelt. Look for it in specialty-food stores or Italian markets. You can use barley in place of farro, and cook according to the package directions.

# farro & tomato salad

**1 Make the farro**
Place the farro in a bowl with 3 cups (24 fl oz/750 ml) water and let stand at room temperature for 2 hours. Drain the farro and place in a saucepan. Add the broth and bring to a boil over medium-high heat. Reduce the heat to medium-low, cover, and simmer until the farro is tender, about 30 minutes. Let stand, covered, for 10 minutes. Transfer to a bowl and let cool to room temperature.

**2 Assemble the salad**
Add the tomatoes and mozzarella to the farro. In a small bowl, whisk together the vinegars, 1 teaspoon salt, and 1/8 teaspoon pepper. Whisk in the oil. Pour the dressing over the salad, add the basil and toss with a fork. Divide among shallow bowls, and serve.

**Farro,** 3/4 cup (4 oz/125 g)

**Vegetable broth,** 2 1/2 cups (20 fl oz/625 ml)

**Plum (Roma) tomatoes,** 2 large, halved lengthwise, seeded and coarsely chopped

**Fresh mozzarella balls (bocconcini),** 1/4 lb (125 g), halved

**Balsamic vinegar,** 2 teaspoons

**Red wine vinegar,** 2 teaspoons

**Salt and freshly ground pepper**

**Olive oil,** 1 tablespoon

**Fresh basil leaves,** 8 large, cut crosswise into thin strips

SERVES 4

65

# endive & radicchio gratin

**Belgian endive (chicory/ witloof),** 4 large heads, halved lengthwise and cut wide ribbons

**Radicchio,** 2 small heads, halved lengthwise and cut into wide ribbons

**Milk,** 1 ½ cups (12 fl oz/ 375 ml)

**Unsalted butter,** 3 tablespoons

**Flour,** 2 tablespoons

**Gruyère or Comté cheese,** 1 cup (2 oz/60 g) shredded

**Salt and freshly ground pepper**

**Parmesan cheese,** ¼ cup (2 oz/60 g) freshly grated

SERVES 4

## 1 Prepare the vegetables

Preheat the oven to 400°F (200°C). Butter a shallow 2-qt (2-l) gratin or baking dish. Add the endive and radicchio to the prepared dish and toss to combine.

## 2 Make the sauce

In a small saucepan over medium heat, warm the milk until small bubbles begin to appear around the edge of the pan. Remove from the heat. In a saucepan over low heat, melt 2 tablespoons of the butter. Add the flour, and whisking to incorporate. Raise the heat to medium-low and cook, stirring often, for 2 minutes. Gradually whisk in the hot milk. Cook, stirring frequently, until the sauce is thick enough to coat the back of a spoon, 3–4 minutes. Add ¾ cup of the Gruyère and stir until it melts. Season to taste with salt and pepper.

## 3 Finish the gratin

Spoon the sauce over the vegetables and dot with the remaining 1 tablespoon butter. Sprinkle with the Parmesan cheese and remaining ¼ cup Gruyère. Bake until the endive is tender, the top of the gratin is golden, about 30 minutes. Serve hot, directly from the pan.

## cook's tip

When making the white sauce be careful not to let the flour burn. For the best results, melt the butter over medium heat and

whisk the flour vigorously. Once golden, continue to whisk and slowly add the hot milk.

## cook's tip

Authentic gumbo uses
okra as a thickener. Instead
of okra, you can substitute
2 tablespoons long-grain rice.
Add it to the pot when you
cook the vegetables.

# kale & red bean gumbo

1 **Cook the vegetables**
Combine the kale, bell pepper, green onions, tomatoes, and broth in a heavy-bottomed saucepan or Dutch oven. Add the bay leaves, oregano, and thyme. Bring to a boil over medium-high heat. Reduce the heat to medium-low, cover, and simmer until the kale is tender, about 30 minutes.

2 **Finish the gumbo**
Add the beans and okra to the vegetables. Cover and cook until the okra is just tender, about 15 minutes for fresh, 5 minutes for frozen. Season to taste with salt, pepper, and hot pepper sauce, if using. Divide the rice among deep bowls and ladle the gumbo atop.

**Kale leaves,** 6 cups (12 oz/ 375 g) chopped

**Green bell pepper (capsicum),** 1, seeded and chopped

**Green (spring) onions,** 1 large, white and pale green parts only, chopped

**Canned tomatoes in purée,** 1 cup (7 oz/220 g)

**Vegetable broth,** 4 cups (32 fl oz/1 l)

**Bay leaves,** 2

**Dried oregano,** 1 teaspoon

**Dried thyme,** 1 teaspoon

**Red beans,** 1 can (15 oz/ 470 g), drained and rinsed

**Fresh okra,** 8 pods, cut into 1/2-inch (12-mm) pieces, or 1 cup frozen okra

**Salt and freshly ground pepper**

**Hot pepper sauce** (optional)

**Steamed white rice,** for serving

SERVES 4

# make more
# to store

# spaghetti with spicy tomato sauce

## SPICY TOMATO SAUCE

**Olive oil,** 2 tablespoons

**Garlic,** 4 large cloves, chopped

**Canned diced plum (Roma) tomatoes,** 4 cans (28 oz/875 g each), drained

**Dried red pepper flakes,** 1 teaspoon

**Salt and freshly ground pepper**

**Salt**

**Spaghetti,** 1 lb (500 g)

**Fresh basil,** ¼ cup (¾ oz/ 20 g) thinly sliced

**Parmesan cheese,** ½ cup (2 oz/60 g) freshly grated, plus shards for garnish

SERVES 4

makes about 7 cups (56 fl oz/1.75 ml) sauce total

Seek out the best-quality canned tomatoes for this robust, spicy sauce. Serve it over spaghetti for dinner tonight and use the rest to prepare baked eggs, eggplant Parmesan, or polenta lasagna.

1 Prepare the sauce
In a large saucepan over medium heat, warm the oil. Add the garlic and sauté for 1 minute. Add the tomatoes and red pepper flakes, raise the heat to high, and bring to a boil. Reduce the heat to medium-low and simmer, uncovered, until the sauce is thick, about 40 minutes. Season to taste with salt and pepper. Remove 5 cups (40 fl oz/1 ml) for storing and let cool (see Storage Tip, right).

2 Cook the pasta
Meanwhile, bring a large pot of water to a boil. Add 2 tablespoons salt and the pasta to the boiling water. Cook, stirring occasionally to prevent sticking, until al dente, according to the package directions. Drain, reserving ½ cup (4 fl oz/ 125 ml) of the cooking water. Add as much of the cooking water as needed to loosen the sauce. Divide the pasta among shallow bowls, top with the sauce and garnish with the basil and Parmesan shards. Pass the remaining grated Parmesan at the table.

## storage tip

Let the sauce cool in the pot, and then spoon it into containers. If using plastic containers, coat the inside with oil or cooking spray to prevent the surface from staining. Refrigerate the sauce for up to 4 days or freeze for up to 1 month.

## cook's tip

Use this tomato sauce with any
style of cooked eggs. Try it over
a simple herb and cheese omelet,
or spoon it over poached eggs
and toasted country bread.

# eggs baked in tomato sauce

**1 Assemble the dish**

Preheat the oven to 400°F (200°C). Lightly coat four 1-cup (8-fl oz/250-ml) ramekins or gratin dishes with oil and place on a baking sheet. In a saucepan over medium heat, warm the tomato sauce. Divide it among the prepared dishes. With the back of a spoon, make 2 indentations in the sauce in each dish. One at a time, break the eggs into small bowl, and then slip into each indentation. Sprinkle with the cheese evenly over the tops of the eggs.

**2 Bake the eggs**

Bake until the eggs are set and the cheese is melted, about 20 minutes. Sprinkle with salt and pepper and serve.

**Spicy Tomato Sauce,** 2 cups (16 fl oz/500 ml), homemade (page 72) or purchased

**Eggs,** 8

**Gouda or provolone cheese,** 1 cup (4 oz/125 g) shredded

**Salt and freshly ground black pepper**

SERVES 4

# baked eggplant parmesan

**Spicy Tomato Sauce,** 2 cups
(16 fl oz/500 ml), homemade
(page 72) or purchased

**Egg,** 1, beaten with
1 tablespoon water

**Dried bread crumbs,** ½ cup
(2 oz/60 g)

**Dried oregano,** ½ teaspoon

**Parmesan cheese,**
2 tablespoons grated

**Salt and freshly ground
pepper**

**Olive oil,** 2 tablespoons

**Eggplant (aubergine),**
2 small, about 1½ lb (750 g),
cut into 8 slices

**Mozzarella cheese,** 1 cup
(4 oz/125 g) shredded

SERVES 4

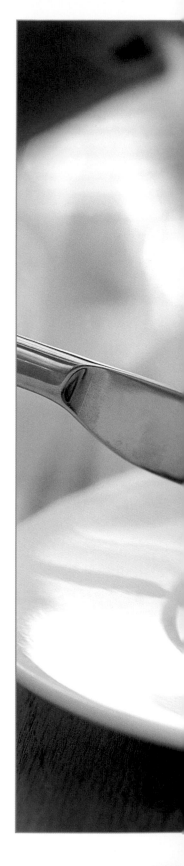

## 1 Prepare the eggplant

Preheat the oven to 400°F (200°C). Place the egg mixture in a wide, shallow dish. Place the bread crumbs in another dish and stir in the oregano, Parmesan, ½ teaspoon salt, and ⅛ teaspoon pepper. In a large frying pan over medium-high heat, warm 1 tablespoon of the oil. Working with 4 eggplant slices at a time, dip a slice in the egg mixture, letting the excess drip back into the bowl. Coat both sides with the bread crumbs and cook, turning once, until browned, about 6 minutes total. Transfer to a plate.

## 2 Assemble the dish

Spoon one-third of the sauce over the bottom of a lightly oiled 9-by-12-inch (23-by-30-cm) square baking dish. Arrange 4 eggplant slices in a single layer in the dish. Spoon one-third of the sauce onto the slices and sprinkle with half of the mozzarella. Top with the remaining eggplant slices and cover with the remaining sauce and mozzarella.

## 3 Bake the eggplant

Bake until the eggplant is tender and the cheese is lightly browned and melted, about 15 minutes. Using a wide spatula, divide among dinner plates, and serve.

## cook's tip

To reduce the bitterness of eggplant, lightly sprinkle the slices with salt and let drain in a colander set over a plate for 30 minutes. Pat with paper towels to remove the salt and bitter juices. Do not rinse under running water, which the eggplant will absorb.

## cook's tip

Capers preserved in salt have
a more intense flavor than those
pickled in vinegar. Look for
salted capers in Italian markets
and specialty-food stores.
Before using salted capers, soak
them in warm water for
about 20 minutes, then drain.

# rigatoni with caponata

## 1 Prepare the sauce

Bring a large pot of water to a boil. In a frying pan over medium-high heat, warm 1 tablespoon of the oil. Add the onion and sauté until translucent, about 4 minutes. Add the remaining oil, the zucchini, and eggplant and cook, stirring occasionally, until the eggplant begins to soften, about 6 minutes. Add the tomato sauce, tomato paste, vinegar, and sugar. Bring to a simmer over medium-high heat. Reduce the heat to medium and cook, uncovered, until the vegetables are tender, about 7 minutes. Stir in the capers and pine nuts, season to taste with salt and pepper, and set aside.

## 2 Cook the pasta

Meanwhile, add 2 tablespoons salt and the pasta to the boiling water. Cook, stirring occasionally to prevent sticking, until al dente, according to the package directions. Drain, reserving ½ cup (4 fl oz/125 ml) of the cooking water. Add the pasta to the sauce and toss to combine. Add as much of the cooking water as needed to loosen the sauce and serve.

**Spicy Tomato Sauce,** 1½ cups (12 fl oz/375 g), homemade (page 72) or purchased

**Olive oil,** 2 tablespoons

**Yellow onion,** 1, chopped

**Zucchini (courgette),** 1 small, quartered lengthwise and sliced

**Eggplant (aubergine),** 1 small, about 1 lb (700 g), cut into ¾-inch (2-cm) cubes

**Tomato paste,** 2 tablespoons, combined with 2 tablespoons warm water

**Red wine vinegar,** 1 tablespoon

**Sugar,** 1 teaspoon

**Capers,** 1 tablespoon, rinsed and drained

**Pine nuts,** 2 tablespoons, toasted

**Salt and freshly ground pepper**

**Rigatoni,** 1 lb (500 g)

SERVES 4

# polenta lasagna

**Spicy Tomato Sauce,** 2 cups (16 fl oz/500 ml), homemade (page 72) or purchased

**Precooked polenta,** 18 oz (560 g), cut into 16 slices

**Fresh ricotta cheese,** ½ cup (4 oz/125 g)

**Pesto,** 2 tablespoons

**Salt and freshly ground pepper**

**Mozzarella cheese,** 6 oz (185 g), cut into 8 slices

SERVES 4

 **Assemble the lasagna**
Preheat the oven to 375°F (190°C). Oil a 9-inch (23-cm) square baking dish. In a small bowl, stir together the ricotta and pesto. Season to taste with salt and pepper. Layer the polenta slices and ricotta mixture in the baking dish. Top with the remaining tomato sauce and then with the mozzarella slices.

2 **Bake the lasagna**
Bake until the cheese is melted and the lasagna is heated through, about 20 minutes. Serve hot, directly from the baking dish.

## cook's tip

Basil pesto is sold in a larger quantity than is needed for this lasagna. To store pesto, spoon tablespoons of it into an ice-cube tray and freeze for later use.

## storage tip

Let the stock cool, then transfer
to airtight containers. Store in the
refrigerator for up to 3 days or
in the freezer for up to 2 months.

# creamy mushroom bisque

The versatile stock includes both fresh and dried mushrooms. It makes a flavorful base for a rich bisque and you'll have enough left over to make a hearty white bean soup or a nutty rice pilaf.

## 1 Make the mushroom stock

In a large saucepan over medium-high heat, warm the oil. Add the onion and sauté until lightly browned, about 15 minutes. Add the mushrooms, celery, and peppercorns along with 2½ qt (2.5 l) water. Bring to a boil, reduce the heat to medium-low, and simmer, uncovered, for 40 minutes. Remove from the heat and let stand for 1 hour. Strain into a bowl, pressing lightly on the solids to extract the liquid, and discard the solids. Reserve 3 cups (24 fl oz/750 ml) of the stock and store the rest (see Storage Tip, left).

## 2 Cook the soup

In a large, heavy saucepan over medium heat, melt the butter. Add the shallot and sauté until translucent, about 2 minutes. Add the cremini mushrooms, cover, and cook until their juices are released, about 3 minutes. Stir in the flour and cook, stirring, until thoroughly blended, about 1 minute. Pour in the reserved stock and the brandy. Bring to a boil, cover, reduce the heat to medium, and simmer for 15–20 minutes.

## 3 Finish the soup

Transfer the soup to a blender and process until puréed. Add the cream and pulse twice. Season to taste with salt and pepper. Ladle into bowls, drizzle with cream, and serve.

### MUSHROOM STOCK

**Olive oil,** 2 tablespoons

**Yellow onion,** 2 large, chopped

**White button mushrooms,** 1½ lb (750 g), sliced

**Dried shiitake or porcini mushrooms,** ½ oz (14 g)

**Celery,** 4 stalks, chopped

**Peppercorns,** 1 teaspoon

**Unsalted butter,** 4 tablespoons (2 oz/60 g)

**Shallot,** 1 large, chopped

**Cremini mushrooms,** 10 oz (315 g), chopped

**Flour,** 3 tablespoons

**Brandy,** ¼ cup (2 fl oz/60 ml)

**Heavy (double) cream,** ½ cup (4 fl oz/125 ml), plus more for garnish

**Salt and freshly ground pepper**

### SERVES 4

makes about 7 cups (56 fl oz/1.75 l) stock total

83

# white bean soup with chard

**Mushroom Stock,** 4 cups
(32 fl oz/1 l) (page 83)

**Olive oil,** 1 tablespoon

**Red onion,** 1 large, chopped

**Leek,** 1, white part only,
halved, rinsed, and sliced

**Garlic,** 1 clove, minced

**Portobello mushrooms,**
3 oz (90 g), stems and gills
removed, and diced

**Dried thyme,** ½ teaspoon

**Swiss chard,** 3 oz (90 g), cut
into strips ½ inch (12 mm)
wide

**Cannellini beans,** 2 cans
(15 oz/470 g each), drained
and rinsed

SERVES 6

1 **Sauté the vegetables**
In a large saucepan over medium-high heat, warm the
oil. Add the onion and leek and sauté until the onions are
translucent, about 4 minutes. Add the garlic, mushrooms,
and thyme and cook, stirring occasionally, until the liquid
released by the mushrooms has evaporated, about 6 minutes.

2 **Finish the soup**
Add the stock, chard, and beans and bring to a boil over
high heat. Reduce the heat to medium-low and simmer,
uncovered, until the chard is just tender, about 8–10 minutes.
Serve immediately.

## cook's tip

To clean a leek quickly, trim off the dark green tops. Cut the stalk in half lengthwise, leaving the root end intact. Rinse the leek under cold running water, separating the layers to remove any embedded dirt. Prepare as directed, removing the root end.

## cook's tip

Regular long-grain or short-grain brown rice can be used in place of basmati. Check the package as the cooking time may vary. Corn kernels and green peas or chopped red bell pepper (capsicum) can be substituted for the broccoli and chickpeas.

# mushroom &
# broccoli pilaf

## 1 Cook the rice

Preheat the oven to 350°F (180°C). In a saucepan over medium heat, warm the stock and sherry until steaming, 8–10 minutes. In a heavy-bottomed ovenproof saucepan or Dutch oven over medium-high heat, melt the butter. Add the onion and sauté until translucent, 4–5 minutes. Add the rice and stir until well coated with the butter, about 1 minute. Pour in the hot broth. Add the thyme, ½ teaspoon salt, and pepper to taste. Bring to a boil, cover, and bake for 35 minutes.

## 2 Finish the pilaf

Remove the rice from the oven and stir in the broccoli and chickpeas. Cover and bake until the broccoli is tender, 10–15 minutes. Let stand, covered, for 5 minutes. Uncover and fluff the pilaf. Transfer to dinner plates, sprinkle with the nuts and red pepper flakes and serve.

**Mushroom Stock,** 2½ cups (20 fl oz/625 ml) (page 83)

**Sherry,** 2 tablespoons

**Unsalted butter,** 2 tablespoons

**Yellow onion,** 1, finely chopped

**Brown basmati rice,** 1 cup (7 oz/220 g)

**Fresh thyme leaves,** 1 tablespoon

**Salt and freshly ground pepper**

**Broccoli,** 1 small head cut into 1-inch (2.5 cm) florets

**Canned chickpeas (garbanzo beans),** 1 cup (7 oz/220 g), rinsed and drained

**Salted roasted cashews,** ½ cup (2 oz/60 g) coarsely chopped

**Red pepper flakes,** pinch

SERVES 4

# lentil salad with feta

### COOKED GREEN LENTILS

**Green lentils,** 1 lb (500 g)

**Carrot,** 1, halved

**Celery,**
1 stalk, cut into 3 pieces

**Yellow onion,** 1, peeled
and halved

**Fresh flat-leaf (Italian),**
about 5 sprigs

**Red onion,** 1, chopped

**Roasted red bell pepper
(capsicum),** 1, seeded and
chopped

**Fresh flat-leaf (Italian)
parsley,** ⅔ cup (1 oz/30 g)
chopped

**Red wine vinegar,**
2 tablespoons

**Olive oil,** 1 tablespoon

**Feta cheese,** ½ cup
(2½ oz/75 g) crumbled

**Salt and freshly ground
pepper**

SERVES 4

makes about 6 cups
(42 oz/1.3 kg) cooked
lentils total

Lentils absorb seasonings and can be transformed
into a variety of distinctive dishes. After making
the cooked lentils for this salad, you can use the
leftovers in a pasta and lentil soup or a spicy curry.

**1 Cook the lentils**
In a large saucepan, combine the lentils, carrot, celery,
yellow onion, parsley sprigs, and 8 cups (64 fl oz/2 l) water.
Bring to a boil over medium-high heat, reduce the heat
to medium-low, cover, and simmer until the lentils are tender
and the liquid has been absorbed, 30–35 minutes. Remove
and discard the vegetables leaving 2½ cups (17½ oz/545 g)
of the lentils for the salad. Set aside the remaining lentils
to cool before storing for later use (see Storage Tip, right).

**2 Prepare the salad**
In a bowl, stir together the red onion, bell pepper,
chopped parsley, and the reserved lentils. Mix in the vinegar
and oil. Add the feta and toss to combine. Season to taste
with salt and pepper and serve.

## storage tip

Store the cooked lentils
in an airtight container in the
refrigerator for up to 3 days.
It is best not to freeze beans.

## cook's tip

You will need to seed and dice the plum (Roma) tomatoes for this recipe. First, use a chef's knife and cut each tomato half lengthwise. Gently squeeze the tomato half over a bowl to remove the seeds and excess liquid. Next, cut each tomato half lengthwise into thin strips. Line up the strips and cut across into a dice. Repeat with the remaining tomato halves.

# sicilian
# lentil soup

## 1 Sauté the vegetables

In a large saucepan over medium-high heat, warm 1 tablespoon of the oil. Add the onion and sauté until translucent, about 4 minutes. Add the remaining 1 tablespoon oil, the garlic, the rosemary, and eggplant, and cook, stirring frequently, until the eggplant is translucent and starts to soften, about 5 minutes.

## 2 Simmer the soup

Add the lentils, pasta, cinnamon, and 6 cups (48 fl oz/ 1.5 l) water. Bring to a boil, reduce the heat to medium-low, and simmer, uncovered, until the eggplant is tender and the pasta is al dente, about 10 minutes. Stir in the tomatoes and season to taste with salt and pepper. Ladle into soup bowls, drizzle with olive oil, and serve.

**Cooked Green Lentils,** 3 cups (21 oz/655 g) (page 88)

**Olive oil,** 2 tablespoons, plus more for drizzling

**Yellow onion,** 1 large, chopped

**Garlic,** 1 clove, minced

**Fresh rosemary,** 1 teaspoon minced

**Eggplant (aubergine),** 1, about 1 lb (700 g), cut into small cubes

**Ditalini, macaroni, or other short pasta,** 1 oz (30 g)

**Ground cinnamon,** 1/4 teaspoon

**Plum (roma) tomatoes,** 2 seeded and chopped

**Salt and freshly ground pepper**

SERVES 4

# lentil, potato & spinach curry

**Cooked Green Lentils,**
2 cups (14 oz/440 g)
(page 88)

**Canola oil,** 2 tablespoons

**Yellow onion,** 1 large,
chopped

**Garlic,** 2 cloves, minced

**Garam masala,**
1 ½ teaspoons

**Ground cumin,** 1 teaspoon

**Ground coriander,**
½ teaspoon

**Red-skinned potatoes,**
2 large, cut in 1-inch (2.5-cm)
cubes

**Baby spinach,** 2 packed
cups (3 oz/90 g)

**Salt and freshly ground
pepper**

**Steamed white or brown
basmati rice,** for serving

**Plain yogurt,** ¼ cup
(2 oz/60 g)

SERVES 4

1 **Sauté the aromatics**
In a heavy-bottomed saucepan or Dutch oven over medium-high heat, warm the oil. Add the onion and sauté until browned, about 8 minutes. Stir in the garlic, garam masala, cumin, coriander, and stir until the spices are toasted and fragrant, about 1 minute.

2 **Cook the vegetables**
Add the potatoes, lentils, and 1 cup (8 fl oz/250 ml) water. Bring to a boil, reduce the heat to medium-low, and simmer, uncovered, until the potatoes are tender, about 10 minutes. Stir in the spinach and cook until it wilts, about 2 minutes. Season to taste with salt and pepper. Spoon the rice into bowls and top with the vegetable curry. Garnish with the yogurt and serve.

## cook's tip

Steamed rice or warmed naan
is an excellent way to round out
the meal. Chopped mustard
greens or kale may be used in
place of the spinach.

# the smarter cook

Whether you are cooking for vegetarians or you simply want to add healthy recipes to your repertoire, you'll find plenty of inspiring dishes for every occasion in this collection. In the following pages, you'll discover tips on how to be a smarter cook, spending less time in the kitchen while still putting a satisfying dinner on the table on even the busiest nights.

Keep your pantry and refrigerator well stocked, and you'll always have the ingredients you need for a quick supper. Put together a weekly menu and shopping list, and you'll make fewer trips to the store. With these simple strategies, you can prepare delicious vegetarian meals in less than 30 minutes. In the following pages, you'll find tips on how to manage your time and organize your kitchen—the keys to becoming a smarter cook.

# get started

You can save time in the kitchen—and avoid extra trips to the store—by writing out your weekly menu and keeping your pantry well stocked. You'll find easy strategies here for planning well-balanced vegetarian dinners, organizing your shopping trips, and maximizing your time in the kitchen. Once you're cooking smarter, you will be able to put together healthy, quick-to-assemble meals any night of the week.

## plan your meals

■ **Look at the whole week.** During the weekend, take time to think about how many meals you'll need to prepare in the week ahead. You'll want to offer variety, mixing up menus such as an Indian-inspired curry with fragrant basmati rice one night, a Creole gumbo with crusty bread on another night, and an Asian stir-fry with a cucumber salad later in the week. If you shop on the weekends, try to plan dishes that require several fresh ingredients for the early days of the week, and save meals that rely primarily on pantry staples for later in the week.

■ **Let the seasons be your guide.** You'll find better quality, fresher ingredients and save money if you shop and cook with the seasons. Imported out-of-season vegetables and fruits are typically more expensive and often lacking in fresh-picked flavor. Plan your menus to match the weather: lighter dishes in the spring and summer, and heartier fare when the days turn cold.

■ **Plan for leftovers.** Make a double batch of a simple recipe such as a soup, stew, or gratin. It takes only a little more time than cooking a smaller portion, and the leftovers are a great time-saver when you need a satisfying dish fast. When you serve the leftovers, try to give them a new look and taste by adding a fresh ingredient or a different garnish or by pairing them with another side dish.

■ **Get everyone involved.** Enlist family members to help you plan the week's menus, so they'll look forward to their suggestions. Then, at dinnertime, recruit them to help with the preparation.

### THINK SEASONALLY

**spring** Make the most of spring's delicately flavored fresh vegetables. Use plenty of leafy green herbs like basil, dill, and mint to season frittatas and creamy pastas. Choose recipes that include new potatoes, asparagus, leeks, and baby spinach.

**summer** Enjoy summer's bounty with juicy tomato salads and fresh corn on the cob. Cook such vegetables as eggplants (aubergines), red onions, zucchini (courgettes) and other summer squash, portobello mushrooms, and bell peppers (capsicums) on the grill.

**autumn** Whole grains studded with nuts and dried fruits pair well with the season's harvest of pumpkin and acorn and butternut squashes. As the vegetables of summer fade, replace them with root vegetables like beets, turnips, parsnips, carrots, and potatoes.

**winter** Hearty soups, ragouts, and risottos satisfy cold-weather appetites. Balance these filling main dishes with crisp salads made from Belgian endive (chicory/witloof), fennel, and radicchio, or with nutrient-rich sautéed or braised greens like kale and chard.

# round it out

Once you have decided what dish to make as the centerpiece of your meal, choose among a wide variety of appealing side dishes to round out the menu. Keep in mind both speed and ease of preparation.

**braised greens** Buy packaged, prewashed greens, such as spinach or mixed braising greens, and cook them in olive oil. For sturdier greens such as kale, add a small amount of broth and cook, covered, until tender.

**cucumbers** Toss sliced cucumbers with vinaigrette and chopped fresh herbs as an accompaniment to sautés and pilafs. Or, dress the slices with rice vinegar, Asian sesame oil, a pinch of sugar, and a sprinkling of toasted sesame seeds to serve alongside Asian dishes.

**fresh vegetables** You can steam or blanch many vegetables ahead of time, refrigerate them, and reheat them at dinnertime. Or, serve the vegetables at room temperature, drizzled with a vinaigrette or with olive oil and lemon juice.

**potatoes** Boil red-skinned potatoes and toss them with butter and chopped chives, parsley, or dill. Serve warm, at room temperature, or chilled. Or, toss with olive oil, sea salt, pepper, and chopped rosemary and roast (see right).

**whole-grain pilafs** Amaranth, quinoa, farro, millet, kasha, and other whole grains make robust, nutritious, side dishes. Sauté the grains with a little canola oil or butter until they release a nutty fragrance. Add simmering water or vegetable broth, cover tightly, and simmer until just tender. Fluff with a fork and let steam, covered, off the heat for a few minutes to finish cooking.

**couscous** Instant couscous, available plain or in a variety of seasoned blends, takes less than 10 minutes to prepare on the stove top and makes a good hot side dish or a cold salad.

**salad** To save time, buy packaged, prewashed greens. Choose salad ingredients that complement the main dish: a salad with lettuce, cucumbers, and an Asian-style dressing to accompany a Thai curry, or an arugula (rocket), tomato, and shaved Parmesan salad dressed with olive oil and lemon juice to serve with an Italian pasta. Make extra dressing and store it in the refrigerator for use throughout the week.

**tomatoes** Arrange ripe tomato slices on a platter. Just before serving, sprinkle with sea salt and coarsely ground pepper and drizzle with a fruity olive oil or an herbed aioli. If desired, tuck fresh basil leaves between the slices and top with crumbled feta cheese or thinly sliced fresh mozzarella.

**roasted vegetables** Cauliflower, asparagus, and bell peppers (capsicums) are well suited to high-heat roasting. Toss the vegetables with a little olive oil, salt, and pepper, and roast in a single layer on a baking sheet at 425°F (220°C) until tender and beginning to brown, 10–20 minutes, stirring occasionally. Root vegetables such as beets, carrots, parsnips, and potatoes can be peeled, cubed, and roasted in a similar manner at 350°F (180°C) for 40–50 minutes.

**simple desserts** Top a scoop of ice cream with berry sauce, chocolate, or caramel. In summer, combine berries and sliced peaches, nectarines, or plums, and drizzle with a flavorite liqueur or top with whipped cream. In the fall and winter, serve poached pears, baked apples, poached dried fruits, or homemade applesauce accompanied with tea biscuits.

# sample menus

These menus are designed to help you plan your weekly meals. Consider your schedule, and then mix and match the main dishes and accompaniments to create the plan that works best for you. Cook double portions of staples like tomato sauce or lentils over the weekend so you can use the leftovers for lunches or dinners later in the week.

| IN MINUTES | WEEKEND SUPPERS | FIT FOR COMPANY |
|---|---|---|
| **Linguine with Creamy Mushroom Sauce** (page 17) | **Chickpea & Sweet Potato Curry** (page 29) | **Wild Mushroom Risotto with Peas** (page 34) |
| Mixed greens with balsamic vinaigrette | Cucumber and cilantro raita | Shaved fennel salad |
| Warm foccacia with herbs and olive oil | Steamed basmati rice | Bread sticks |
| **Tofu Stir-Fry with Black Bean Sauce** (page 25) | **Spicy Corn Cakes with Black Beans** (page 38) | **Spring Vegetable Tart** (page 53) |
| Steamed jasmine rice | Warm corn tortillas | Butter lettuce and avocado salad with Champagne vinaigrette |
| **Red Pepper & Goat Cheese Frittata** (page 14) | Jicama and red pepper salad with lime vinaigrette | **Pappardelle with Zucchini & Lemon** (page 13) |
| Roasted asparagus | **Grilled Portobello Burgers** (page 45) | Sliced tomatoes with basil and olive oil |
| Herbed biscuits | Oven-roasted potato wedges | Garlic crostini |
| **Spanish Bean Stew** (page 46) | Mixed salad greens with vinaigrette | **Asparagus Milanese** (page 22) |
| Grilled cheese and tomato sandwiches | **Baked Eggplant Parmesan** (page 76) | Sauteed sliced red potatoes with butter and herbs |
| **Miso Soup with Udon Noodles** (page 26) | Baby spinach salad with sliced mushrooms and Balsamic vinaigrette | Arugula and Parmesan salad with red wine vinaigrette |
| Purchased vegetable sushi rolls | **Endive & Radicchio Gratin** (page 66) | **Potato and Gruyère Tartlets** (page 54) |
| Cucumber salad with rice wine vinagrette | Steamed asparagus | Steamed artichokes with melted lemon-butter |
| | Roasted butternut squash | |

# shortcut meals

On those days when you don't have time to cook, well-stocked supermarkets or delicatessens can provide lots of tasty, wholesome items to fill out your menu. Here are several easy-to-fix dishes that can be made at the last minute when you need a quick meal or filling snack.

■ **Marinated tofu** Pressed, marinated, and baked, these ready-to-eat tofu squares make a great base for a sandwich, salad, or vegetable stir-fry. Found in the refrigerated section of the supermarket, they are available in a variety of flavors and are an excellent source of protein.

■ **Hummus** Prepared hummus is widely available in supermarkets. Dress it up with a squeeze of fresh lemon juice and a drizzle of extra-virgin olive oil. Toast whole-wheat pita and fill it with hummus, shredded carrot, tomato slices, and store-bought tahini. Or, as a part of a Mediterranean salad plate, serve hummus alongside olives, feta cheese, stuffed grape leaves, and cherry tomatoes.

■ **Eggs** It's a good idea to keep a supply of eggs on hand. Make a quick frittata (page 14) and serve it with toasted bread and a green salad dressed with vinaigrette, or prepare a simple omelet using chopped leftover vegetables and cheese and serve it with sautéed potatoes.

■ **Pizza crusts** Partially baked pizza crusts can be quickly transformed into a simple supper or a snack. Top with a prepared sauce, leftover vegetables, and grated cheese and bake in a 450°F (230°C) oven until the crust is heated through and the cheese is melted.

■ **Pasta** Always stock the pantry with a few packages of pasta and jars of pasta sauce. Add crumbled vegetarian sausages or cubes of marinated baked tofu to the sauce for flavor and texture, or stir in leftover cooked greens, roasted red peppers (capsicums), and sliced olives. Top the sauced pasta with freshly grated Parmesan for a hearty supper.

■ **Burritos** Keep flour tortillas in the refrigerator for preparing burritos or soft tacos using cheese, salsa, rice, and canned refried pinto or black beans. Warm the tortilla, fill with the ingredients, and roll up to eat.

# shop smarter

Using high-quality ingredients will give you a head start on memorable meals. Look for a produce store, specialty-food shop, and grocery store that you can rely on for first-rate foods and dependable service. If possible, call ahead and place your order, so it's ready to pick up on your way home from work. Also stop by your local farmers' market regularly to stay current with what's in season.

■ **Produce** Look for organic or locally grown produce when possible, for better flavor and healthier eating. Greens and herbs should be brightly colored and have no dark edges or limp or yellowed leaves. Root vegetables like carrots and beets should feel solid, and other vegetables, such as cucumbers, eggplants (aubergines), and zucchini (courgettes), should be firm to the touch and have taut skins. Pass up onions, garlic, and potatoes with any signs of sprouting, and avoid potatoes with a greenish tinge. If there is a farmers' market in your area, get in the habit of visiting it once a week to stay in touch with what's in season and to take advantage of good deals on bumper-crop fruits and vegetables.

■ **Tofu** Bean curd is available packed in water or sealed in vacuum-packed aseptic boxes. Always check the expiration date before purchasing; water-packed tofu is more perishable than aseptic-packed tofu. For stir-fries and soups, look for medium or firm tofu, which holds its shape in slices or cubes. For sandwich fillings, dips, or desserts, use soft or silken tofu.

■ **Broth** Good-quality vegetable broth can be found in cans and aseptic boxes on supermarket shelves. Read the labels carefully to avoid unwholesome ingredients and, if possible, purchase organic brands for both better health and optimal flavor. It's best to avoid vegetable broths that contain carrots as a primary ingredient, as these products give finished dishes an orange cast.

■ **Grains** If you live near a good natural foods store, look for whole grains sold in bulk. When purchasing packaged grains, always check expiration dates. Grains should have a fresh, slightly nutty smell. Avoid musty or rancid odors or a clumpy, stringy appearance.

---

## MAKE A SHOPPING LIST

**prepare in advance** Make a list of ingredients you need to buy before you go shopping.

**make a template** Create a list template on your computer, then fill it in during the week before you go shopping.

**categorize your lists** Use these categories to keep your lists organized: pantry, fresh, and occasional.

■ **pantry items** Check the pantry and write down any items that need to be restocked.

■ **fresh ingredients** These are for immediate use and include produce, dairy products, tofu, and some cheeses. You might need to visit different stores or supermarket sections, so divide the list into subcategories.

■ **occasional items** This revolving list is for refrigerated items that are replaced as needed, such as butter, milk and eggs.

**be flexible** Be ready to change your menus based on the freshest ingredients at the market.

**food processor** A miniprocessor is useful for chopping small amounts of garlic, parsley, or other herbs. A standard-sized processor with a 12- to 14-cup (3- to 3.5-l) capacity is handy for making pesto, chopping onions, grating cheese or carrots, and puréeing dips as well as other foods.

**grill pan** This ridged cast-iron pan is used on the stove top and produces attractive cross-hatching and nearly the same taste as cooking on an outdoor grill. To ensure that food is well seared, always let the pan preheat over high heat for about 5 minutes before adding food to it.

**microplane** Available in various sizes, shapes, and degrees of fineness, these handheld, easy-to-use graters are unsurpassed for fast-and-easy grating of hard cheese, chocolate, citrus zest, and fresh ginger.

**salad spinner** Whether your spinner uses a pump, crank, or pull cord, the centrifugal force whirling salad greens will ensure a crisp, dry salad. Depending on the style of your spinner, the basket can also serve as a colander for rinsing the salad greens.

**wok** With its generous size, sloping sides, and rounded bottom, a wok is the ideal implement for cooking Asian stir-fries. The shape and depth of the pan guarantees that all the ingredients will be exposed to the hot surface and that they can be tossed and stirred without fear of them spilling over the rim.

# make the most of your time

Once you've planned your weekly menus, you can start strategizing about how to make the most of your time. Get your shopping and prep work done in advance and you'll be ready to cook at dinnertime.

- **Stock up** Avoid last-minute shopping trips by keeping your pantry well stocked. Make a note on your shopping list whenever you're getting low on any staple, and replace it the next time you go to the store. Keep a good supply of basic nonperishable ingredients on hand, so you can always improvise a simple meal or side dish.

- **Shop less** Write out your shopping list as you put together your weekly meal plan and then check your pantry. By planning carefully, you can pick up all the staples that you'll need for the week in one trip.

- **Do it ahead** Prep as many ingredients as you can when you have extra time. Wash, peel, and chop vegetables and store them in resealable bags or airtight containers. Make up marinades or salad dressings and store them in the refrigerator. Cook extra side dishes, such as rice, polenta, or steamed vegetables, and store in airtight containers in the refrigerator. Check your ingredients and tools the night before, so you'll be able to find everything easily when you start to cook.

- **Double up** Make extra for the next night. Wisely used, leftovers can be a great asset to a busy cook. But don't serve a warmed-over version of the same exact dish the next night. Instead of doubling a whole recipe, cook only the recipe's foundation, without the accompanying sauces or additional flavorings. At a subsequent meal, you can present the main ingredient with a different sauce or seasonings.

- **Cook smarter** Read through the recipe from start to finish before you begin. Visualize the techniques and go through the recipe step-by-step in your mind. Clear your counters and make sure the kitchen is clean and neat before you start. If you have friends or family around to help, assign specific tasks, such as peeling carrots, chopping onions, making the salad, or setting the table.

# the well-stocked kitchen

Smart cooking is all about being organized. Keeping your pantry, refrigerator, and freezer well stocked and neat means you'll save time when you are ready to prepare a meal. Once you're in the habit of keeping track of the ingredients in your kitchen, you'll find that you can shop less frequently and spend less time in the store when you do.

On the pages that follow, you'll find an easy-to-use guide to all the ingredients you'll need to make the recipes in this book, along with dozens of tips on how to organize and store them properly. Check to see what's in your kitchen now, then all you have to do is make a list, go shopping, and fill your shelves. Once your kitchen is organized and stocked, you'll spend less time cooking and have more time to enjoy your family and friends around the table.

# the pantry

Typically, the pantry is a closet or one or more cupboards where you store canned and jarred foods, dried herbs and spices, oils and vinegars, grains and noodles, and such fresh foods as potatoes, onions, garlic, ginger, and shallots. Make sure that your pantry is cool, dry, and dark, as direct heat and light cause herbs and spices to lose their intensity and hasten the rancidity of grains and oils.

## stock your pantry

- Take inventory of your pantry using the Pantry Staples list.

- Remove everything from the pantry; clean the shelves and reline with paper, if needed; and then resort the items by type.

- Discard items that have passed their expiration date or have a stale or otherwise questionable appearance.

- Make a list of items that you need to replace or stock.

- Shop for the items on your list.

- Restock the pantry, organizing items by type so everything is easy to find.

- Write the purchase date on perishable items and clearly label bulk items.

- Keep staples you use often toward the front of the pantry.

- Keep dried herbs and spices in their containers and preferably in a dedicated spice or herb organizer, shelf, or drawer.

## keep it organized

- Look over the recipes in your weekly menu plan and check your pantry to make sure you have all the ingredients you'll need.

- Rotate items as you use them, moving the oldest ones to the front of the pantry so they will be used first.

- Keep a list of the items you use up so that you can replace them.

---

### QUICK MARINADES

When you have fresh food on hand, but you're short on time, here are some quick-and-easy seasoning ideas from the pantry. Simply season vegetables or tofu to taste with one of the following seasonings, then grill, broil, or pan-fry, and dinner is served.

**INFUSED OILS**
- Chile-infused oil
- Herb-infused oil
- Garlic-infused oil

**SPICE MIXTURES**
- Garam masala
- Curry powder
- Creole seasoning
- Chili powder (serve with lime)

**VINEGARS & VINAIGRETTES**
- Balsamic vinegar
- Flavored vinegars
- Purchased vinaigrette

**OTHER**
- Dried ground mushrooms, such as porcini, chanterelle, or shiitake
- Sesame seeds
- Crushed fennel seeds
- Herbes de Provence

## PANTRY STORAGE

**dried herbs & spices**  Dried herbs and spices start losing flavor after about 6 months. Buy them in small quantities, store in airtight containers labeled with the purchase date, and replace often.

**oils**  Store unopened bottles of oil at room temperature in a cool, dark place. Oils will keep for up to 1 year, but their flavor diminishes over time. Store opened bottles for 3 months at room temperature or in the refrigerator for up to 6 months.

**grains & pasta**  Store grains in airtight containers for up to 3 months, checking occasionally for signs of rancidity or infestation. The shelf life of most dried pastas is 1 year. Although they are safe to eat beyond that time, they will have lost flavor and might be brittle. Once you open a package, put the pasta you don't cook into an airtight container.

**fresh pantry foods**  Store your fresh pantry items—garlic, onions, shallots, and some roots and tubers—in a cool, dark place, check them occasionally for sprouting or spoilage, and discard if necessary. Never store potatoes next to onions; when placed next to each other, they produce gases that hasten spoilage. Store citrus fruits uncrowded and uncovered on a countertop.

**canned foods**  Discard canned foods if the can shows any signs of expansion or buckling. Once you have opened a can, transfer any unused portion to an airtight container or resealable plastic bag and refrigerate or freeze.

## PANTRY STAPLES

### DRIED HERBS & SPICES

cayenne pepper

chili powder

curry powder

ginger

paprika

red pepper flakes

### OILS

Asian sesame

canola

olive

### VINEGARS

balsamic

red wine

sherry

### CANNED & JARRED

beans: red, chickpeas (garbanzo beans), kidney, pinto

capers

coconut milk

roasted red peppers (capsicums)

tomatoes: diced, whole in purée

tomato paste

### MISCELLANEOUS

baking soda (bicarbonate of soda)

cornstarch (cornflour)

dried bread crumbs

dried porcini mushrooms

flour

green lentils

vegetable broth

### GRAINS & NOODLES

Asian wheat noodles

cornmeal

couscous

dried pasta

*farro*

quick-cooking polenta

rice: Arborio, basmati, wild rice

### CONDIMENTS

chili paste

hot pepper sauce

soy sauce

whole-grain mustard

### DRIED FRUITS & NUTS

almonds

cashews

cranberries

pine nuts

### FRESH FOODS

avocado

fresh ginger

garlic

onions

potatoes

shallots

tomatoes

winter squash

### SPIRITS

sake

sherry

white wine

# the refrigerator & freezer

Once you have stocked and organized your pantry, you can apply the same time-saving principles to your refrigerator and freezer. Used for short-term cold storage, the refrigerator is ideal for keeping vegetables, fruits, dairy products, tofu, and leftovers fresh. Proper freezing will preserve most of the flavor in many prepared dishes for several months.

## general tips

- Foods lose flavor under refrigeration, so proper storage and an even temperature of below 40°F (5°C) are important.

- Freeze foods at 0°F (-18°C) to retain color, texture, and flavor.

- Don't crowd foods in the refrigerator. Air should circulate freely to keep foods evenly cooled.

- To prevent freezer burn, use only moistureproof wrappings, such as aluminum foil, airtight plastic containers, or resealable plastic bags.

## leftover storage

- You can store most cooked dishes in an airtight container in the refrigerator for up to 4 days or in the freezer for up to 4 months.

- Most grain, bean, or potato-based salads can be stored in an airtight container in the refrigerator for up to 4 days. Salads made with fresh vegetables do not freeze well.

- Check the contents of the refrigerator at least once a week and promptly discard old or spoiled food.

- Let food cool to room temperature before storing it in the refrigerator or freezer. Transfer the cooled food to an airtight plastic or glass container, leaving room for expansion if freezing. Or, put the cooled food into a resealable plastic freezer bag, expelling as much air as possible before sealing the bag closed.

### KEEP IT ORGANIZED

**clean first** Remove items a few at a time and wash the refrigerator thoroughly with warm, soapy water, then rinse well with clear water. Wash and rinse your freezer at the same time.

**rotate items** Check the expiration dates on refrigerated items and discard any that have exceeded their time. Toss out any items that have off odors or look questionable.

**stock up** Use the list on the opposite page as a starting point to decide what items you need to buy or replace.

**shop** Shop for the items on your list.

**date of purchase** Label items that you plan to keep for more than a few weeks, writing the date directly on the package or on a piece of masking tape.

### WINE STORAGE

Once a wine bottle is uncorked, the wine is exposed to air, eventually causing it to taste like vinegar. Store opened wine in the refrigerator for up to 3 days.

# fresh herb & vegetable storage

■ Trim the stem ends of a bunch of parsley, stand the bunch in a glass of water, drape a plastic bag loosely over the leaves, and refrigerate. Wrap other fresh herbs in a damp paper towel, slip into a plastic bag, and store in the crisper. Rinse and stem all herbs just before using.

■ Store tomatoes and eggplants (aubergines) at room temperature.

■ Cut about ½ inch (12 mm) off the end of each asparagus spear; stand the spears, tips up, in a glass of cold water; and refrigerate, changing the water daily. The asparagus will keep for up to 1 week.

■ Rinse leafy greens such as chard, dry in a salad spinner, wrap in damp paper towels, and store in a resealable plastic bag in the refrigerator crisper for up to 1 week. Store other vegetables in resealable bags in the crisper and rinse before using. Sturdy vegetables will keep for up to 1 week, and more delicate ones for only a few days.

# cheese storage

■ Wrap all cheeses well to prevent them from drying out. Hard cheeses, such as Parmesan, have a low moisture content, so they keep longer than fresh cheeses, such as feta or *queso fresco*. Use fresh cheeses within a couple of days. Store soft and semisoft cheeses for as long as 2 weeks and hard cheeses for up to 1 month.

# soy product storage

■ Once the original tofu packaging has been opened, drain and rinse the tofu, and then again drain, rinsed, and pack it into an airtight container. Add fresh water to cover the tofu completely, cover the container, and refrigerate. Change the water daily. The tofu will keep for up to 1 week

■ Fresh edamame is best used within 24 hours of buying. However, wrapped tightly in plastic wrap it can be refrigerated for up to 2 weeks and placed in the freezer for up to 2 months.

# index

# weldon**owen**

415 Jackson Street, Suite 200, San Francisco, CA 94111
www.wopublishing.com

## MEALS IN MINUTES SERIES

Conceived and produced by Weldon Owen Inc.
Copyright © 2007 by Weldon Owen Inc. and Williams-Sonoma, Inc.

The recipes in this book have been previously
published as *Vegetarian* in the Food Made Fast series.

All rights reserved, including the right of reproduction
in whole or in part in any form.

Printed by 1010 Printing in China

Set in Formata
This edition first printed in 2011
10 9 8 7 6 5 4 3 2 1

Library of Congress Cataloging-in-Publication
data is available.

Weldon Owen is a division of
## BONNIER

**Photographer**  Bill Bettencourt
**Food Stylist**  Kevin Crafts
**Photographer's Assistant**  Angelica Cao
**Food Stylist's Assistant**  Alexa Hyman
**Text Writer**  Stephanie Rosenbaum

## ACKNOWLEDGMENTS

Weldon Owen wishes to thank the following people
for their generous support in producing this book:
Heather Belt, Ken DellaPenta, Judith Dunham, Denise Lincoln,
Lesli Neilson, Sharon Silva, Jen Straus, and Victoria Woolard.

Photograph by Tucker + Hossler: page 45

ISBN-13: 978-1-61628-256-1
ISBN-10: 1-61628-256-8

## A NOTE ON WEIGHTS AND MEASURES

All recipes include customary U.S. and metric measurements. Metric conversions are based on
a standard developed for these books and have been rounded off. Actual weights may vary.